The Blue Day Book for Kids

The Blue Day Book
for Kids

Bradley Trevor Greive

Andrews McMeel
Publishing

Kansas City

05 06 07 08 09 WKT 10 9 8 7 6 5 4

ISBN: 0-7407-5023-2

Library of Congress Control Number: 2004113727

Book design by Holly Camerlinck
Children's literature editorial consultant: Patrick Regan

Attention: Schools and Businesses

Andrews McMeel books are available at quantity discounts with bulk purchase for educational, business, or sales promotional use. For information, please write to: Special Sales Department, Andrews McMeel Publishing, 4520 Main Street, Kansas City, Missouri 64111.

Photo Credits
Australian Picture Library www.australianpicturelibrary.com.au
Austral International www.australphoto.com.au
Getty Images www.gettyimages.com
Photolibrary.com www.photolibrary.com
Stock Photos www.stockphotos.com.au

Credit details for the remarkable photographers whose work appears in *The Blue Day Book for Kids* and other books by Bradley Trevor Greive are freely available at www.btgstudios.com.

The Blue Day Book
for Kids

Have you ever had a blue day?

A blue day is a day when nothing goes right
and you feel kind of lousy.

You might feel grumpy,

lonely,

really shy,

or just plain pooped.

Basically, you're not much fun to be around.

Other people may not understand how you feel. In fact, on blue days it seems like everyone is ignoring you

 or picking on you!

A blue day can sneak up on you
when you don't expect it.

Someone might do or say something mean
that hurts your feelings,

or you might make a silly mistake and feel weird about it.
(And trying to cover it up only makes things worse!)

 Your parents may be mad at you or even yell at you,

or you might get put in time-out at school—
that's a sure way to a blue day!

Have you ever been forced to share your favorite toy
or snack when you really didn't want to?
(Grown-ups don't always understand
how hard it is to share.)

Or had to eat Brussels sprouts for dinner? Blecch!
(How come no one makes you share
your Brussels sprouts?)

Does it ever seem like you're too big to play
with the little kids but too little to play with the big kids?

Feeling like you don't fit in
can really bring on a blue day,

 which is like being sick but not knowing what hurts.

Everything seems impossible on a blue day.

You don't feel like playing

or laughing

or even talking.

On a blue day, it's like you're stuck in a deep hole,
and you can't climb out.

Well, listen up, kid! You *can* get past a blue day—
there are lots of ways to do it.

Sometimes just a little nap can make you
feel better and help you see things clearly.

But if you don't feel like resting, try singing
your favorite songs as loud as you can.

And while you're at it, break out some
wild dance moves!

 If you don't feel like hanging out with friends,
you can have some fun on your own.

Try to stand on your head—
it's a great way to see the world differently.
(More grown-ups should try this.)

By the way, did you ever stop to think
that everyone on the other side of the world
is walking around upside down? Weird, huh?

Another great way to beat a blue day is to be creative.
Get out the paints, crayons, and spaghetti sauce
and cut loose!

Shake up your usual routine and try something you've never done before

or pretend you're someone else entirely.

Sometimes you can cheer up by talking
to your best friends or even just thinking about
someone you really like. It's true,

especially if you think about a time
you did something really crazy together.

Aha, you see—a smile can sneak up on you
just like a blue day can.

Before you know it, you'll be back to your old self. In fact, if you're not careful, you might start smiling so much people will think you're up to something.

 Of course, you *are* up to something. You're cheering yourself up by changing the color of your day.

With a little imagination, you can change a blue day
into a new day, a day when all kinds of
amazing things might happen,

a day when it's great to be you!

Now, isn't that a much better way to look at the world?

Yeah, I think so, too.